AF507516

FULFILLING THE FAITH

The Ultimate Guide to Answering The Call Of God, Getting Into Alignment with Your Authentic Self, and Living A Purposeful Life.

Venise D. Allen

ALSO BY VENISE D. ALLEN

It's Your Time to Rise: 120 Motivational Notes to Empower You on Your Journey to Transforming Your Life.

TABLE OF CONTENTS

INTRODUCTION

Are you seeking a deeper, more meaningful relationship with Jesus Christ?

It may seem strange and unimaginable that so many people who have joined the Christian faith and devoted themselves to being a Christian are still groping to understand their life's meaning and purpose for existing.

So many have spent years in fellowship, doing great things for themselves and others, and have been instrumental in great works in the church, yet they are still dissatisfied with their life.

Often they may become so hardened in the belief that this is just the way the life of a Christian should be and that it doesn't get any better than what exists for them on earth. Others sit around, waiting for their transformation to "fall out of the sky." And then some Christians are waiting to die to live an incredible life in heaven.

Here is the issue; every individual has been given a unique life for a valuable purpose to fulfill as they are on this earth. Instead of living their lives in the unique way God has designed them, they have set themselves aside to practice an impersonal way of being a believer. They have removed themselves-their identity and blueprint from living. They have taken on a life where they allow others, such as parents and family members, society, social media, spiritual leaders, pastors, trends and seasons, and other circumstances, to determine who they are and give them rules and guidelines on how to live their lives as Christians. The element of their divine identity is left out of the equation, and this causes them to be disconnected from God, the creator and the source of all existence.

When you are disconnected from God, you will grope with understanding the meaning of your life and the purpose of your existence. Being disconnected will cause you to be dissatisfied with your life and settle for mediocrity in or less. You will live with unfulfillment, emptiness, sorrow, regret, and void of reality.

You need to realize this; life is a spiritual journey lived in this physical world and requires you to process and make sense of your physical experiences so that you can learn, grow and evolve, thereby fulfilling your God-given purpose on this earth. Life requires that you live in such a way that your spiritual identity, true essence, and work leave an impact that creates change for others. Life is a journey meant to be lived fully, causing you to expand to fulfill your purpose and destiny. Life is about unveiling who you are in Jesus Christ, not necessarily what you do. Therefore, even though you are a believer, regardless of how long you are a part of the faith, if you are experiencing any form of dissatisfaction or have questions regarding your life's journey, you must see it as a call from God to get into alignment with His vision and will for your life. You should no longer live by your will, the will of those around you and your society, or their intellect and beliefs about you. It is time for you to surrender and seek God for yourself.

The purpose of this book, Fulfilling the Faith, is to provide a guide to understanding and answering the call of God in your life. This book will assist you in getting into alignment with your authentic self to maximize your unique contribution to life, your profession of faith in God, and your purpose in the world. By following the guide in this book and investing your time and resources in following the different stages, you will develop a deeper, more meaningful relationship with Jesus Christ.

In the pages to come, you will be reintroduced to God's ultimate purpose for your life. You will learn of His love for humanity and how He transmuted His passion into purpose with the element of forgiveness. You will also learn how to apply this love to determine your purpose.

You will discover the nature of your calling and the caller who calls you, why you are called, and the types of calling that will ultimately bring you to fulfilling your destiny.

You will also receive clarity about your potential and learn the art of perseverance through the cost of following the call. Finally, you will receive information on understanding and creating the archetype of a purposeful life.

At the end of each chapter, there are affirmations to challenge negative thoughts and strengthen your belief in God and your purpose for existence. You should also seek to discuss your concerns and further need for clarification with your pastors or spiritual leaders.

Finally, there is no single path, pre-established way, or set timeline for you to get into alignment with God's will for your life; however, there is a unique assignment for your life that you are required to accomplish before leaving this earth. This assignment is between you and God. While others can help to guide you into uncovering and fulfilling your work, it is your responsibility to pursue, achieve and accomplish. At the end of this book, I desire that you will:

- Be courageous in your pursuit of God's purpose for your life.
- Be fearless in standing for your authenticity and purpose in Christ.
- Be resolute in cultivating your purposeful life through an intimate relationship with Jesus Christ.
- Be transformational and impactful in your environment through the leading of the Holy Spirit and
- Fulfill your destiny in God.

It's your journey; let God be pleased. Let God get all the Glory.

PART ONE

YOUR PURPOSE IS LOVE

Beloved, let us love one another, for love is of God, and
everyone who loves is born of God and knows God.
1 John 4:7

1

AWAKENING TO THE POWER OF LOVE

God loves you. God loves you so much that He created you. God loves you so much that He established an effective plan for your life. God loves you so much that He is here with you. God loves you so much that He wants to dwell permanently within you to give you hope and a future.

I know this is hard to believe because your life encounters may not allow you to experience the truth of God's love. But what if I told you that your life encounters are a part of the plan to allow you to feel and experience God's love and also to share this love with others?

The book of Genesis begins with the story of creation. It tells us that God created man, Adam, in His image and likeness. After creating Adam and assigning him duties in His garden, God saw it fit that He made a woman to be his helpmate. Adam and Eve were responsible for taking authority over God's creation. Of all the instructions God gave them, there was one command that they were required to obey. In the middle of the Garden of Eden were the Tree of Life and the Tree of Knowledge of Good and Evil. God willed them not to eat from the tree of the knowledge of good and evil, for when they eat from it, they will undoubtedly die.

The scripture tells us that the crafty serpent came to Eve and influenced her to disobey God by eating fruit from the forbidden tree. Eve saw that the fruit was good, took some, ate, and gave Adam to partake. After being deceived, they realized they were no longer covered and made coverings themselves. They also hid from God when God called them because they knew they had done something wrong.

For acts of disobedience, there are repercussions. You could consider this a universal law. First, the serpent was cursed by God for the evil it did in deceiving Eve. Second, God cursed Eve to feel severe pains in childbearing, and with painful labor, she will give birth to children. Eve was also cursed with the desire for her husband, and the husband will rule over her. And so it is for every woman because of Eve. For Adam, God cursed the ground and made it difficult so that he could only eat food from it through painful toil throughout his life. Men, through Adam, were cursed with hard work until the day they died and returned to the ground.

Because of Adam and Eve's disobedience and the curse God placed upon them, they could no longer dwell in the garden, the special place created for them. Their disobedience caused them to become aware of and experience the difference between good and evil. God acknowledged that man, knowing good and evil, was like God. Because of the curse they received, God was merciful enough not to let them remain in the garden, for indeed, they would have eaten from the Tree of Life, and this would cause them to live forever under their curse.

Adam and Eve were clothed by God and placed outside the garden. They were still the ultimate objects of God's love; however, because they were now "like God," knowing good and evil, they had to go live in the land where they would contend for their existence and, after a while, would die to be released from their curse.

Adam and Eve's exposure created a struggle between committing to fellowshipping with the Almighty God and indulging in evil. Unfortunately, humans on their own are not strong enough to fight evil, so they succumb to the world's evils as opposed to clinging to fellowship with God and obedience in following His will. Evils can be described as idolatry, physical and sexual abuse, various pain such as physical and mental illnesses, suffering, multiple forms of oppression, stagnancy, greed, separation of families, disinheritance, corruption in high places, famine, and drought, among other inhumane conditions that affect individuals on a more personal level and global level.

Regardless of the evils in our world and what may have affected us individually, God still has an effective plan for our lives and desires to dwell within us. For this reason, God also included the curse to the serpent, the deceiver and evil one, "I will put enmity between you and the woman and between your offspring and hers; he will crush your head, and you will strike his heel" (Genesis 3:15). This meant that because of what Adam and Eve did, God knew what evil fate awaited us. Therefore, to help us overcome the evil fate, He made sure that there was a redemptive plan for us to be reconciled to Him. In other words, we can overcome all the evil that has happened to us and replace it with good.

To demonstrate the redemptive plan, which emphasizes God's love towards us, God allowed Jesus Christ, His only begotten son, a man without sin and undeserving of His death, to die for us so we could be reconciled to Him.

It does not matter about our age. It does not matter what experiences we have undergone. It does not matter what we have done. It does not matter our race or ethnicity or if we've previously worshipped another god. Jesus Christ's death allows us all the opportunity to overcome evil with good and live a victorious life here on earth.

Scriptural Affirmations

- God made a way for me to overcome sin. Genesis 3:15.
- Jesus Christ died for me. Romans 5:8.
- Jesus Christ suffered so I could be healed from my sins. Isaiah 53:5.
- Jesus Christ is with me and within me. Isaiah 7:14.
- I am sanctified by God. 1 John 3:20.
- I shall humble myself before the Almighty God. Psalms 138:6.
- God's plans for my life are to prosper, protect, give me hope, and give me a better future. Jeremiah 29:11.
- What the enemy did to me to hurt me, God intended it for good, to accomplish what is now being done. Through me, God will save many lives. Genesis 50:20.
- I am blessed, and I am a blessing. Genesis 12:3.
- The Lord shall direct my heart into His love and Christ's perseverance. 2 Thessalonians 3:5.
- I shall overcome evil with good. Romans 12:21.
- No weapon formed against me shall prevail. Every tongue that rises against me I will condemn. Isaiah 54:17.

TRANSMUTING LOVE INTO PURPOSE

Love is often described as a deep, intense, passionate, and tender feeling for another individual. The feeling of love is evident in the show of affection, attachment, and devotion to the individual who is being loved. In the Bible, in 1st Corinthians 13:4-18, the apostle Paul explains, "Love is patient, love is kind. It does not envy; it does not boast. It is not proud. It does not dishonor others, is not self-seeking, is not easily angered, it keeps no record of wrongs. Love does not delight in evil but rejoices with the truth. It always protects, always trusts, hopes, and perseveres. Love never fails".

From this, we can see that love is a supernatural force or energy that is felt strongly and, when felt, is transmuted into action that can be seen and experienced by our desired recipients. Love emanates through thoughts, feelings, emotions, words, and actions. The profession of love allows for trust, care, respect, provision, commitment, and devotion.

This is the Love God has for us. Even when we sin and fall short of His glory, He promises to forgive us when we seek His forgiveness. To receive His forgiveness, God created a process so every individual could have equal access.

The Process of Forgiveness

The old testament law required that almost everything be cleansed with blood. This included the sins of humanity (Hebrews 9:22). The bible tells us that the wage of sin is death (Romans 6:23). This meant that something had to die to pay for our sins, hence, the use of animals as sacrifices for sins instead of the individual with the sin. The animals used for atonement had to be undefiled, without defects and blemishes. The individual who was going to shed the animal's blood had to identify with the animal before killing it. By faith, as the animal is inflicted with death, the sinner would consider and believe his sins were forgiven and wiped away.

This practice was temporary, and the ritual had to be performed repeatedly because of man's constant struggle with sin. Animals for sacrifice would eventually become scarce, and the debt of sin would grow exponentially.

Because of God's love towards us and His desire to see humans get into alignment with His will for our lives, He, according to 2nd Corinthians 5:21, "made Him (Jesus) who had no sin to be sin for us so that in Him we might become the righteousness of God." Jesus Christ became the substitute for the spotless animal. He never sinned but was made to represent all sins of past, present, and future generations, including you and me. Jesus became the ultimate sacrifice that through repentance, human beings can receive complete forgiveness and become the righteousness of God.

God could have given up on us. God could have destroyed all of us. God could have allowed humanity to continue in their sin and suffering forever, but He saw it fit to give us, every human being, an opportunity to repent and be saved. Because of this great sacrifice, Jesus Christ declared a great commission for us to follow in response to God's love.

In Matthew 22:36-40 Jesus was asked, "Teacher, which is the greatest commandment in the Law?" to this question, Jesus replied, "Love the Lord your God with all your heart and with all your soul and all your mind. This is the first and greatest commandment. And the second is like it: Love your neighbor as yourself. All the Law and the prophets hang on these two commandments."

To love God is to accept the benefits of His sacrifice for us and apply them to our lives. These include forgiveness of our sins, compassion for the difficulties we experience, and lack of knowledge for things we have done unaware. Jesus's death sacrifice benefits include grace, mercy, peace, patience, favor, and acceptance. The gifts you receive from Jesus's death do not take the pain and hurt away. However, it gives you a different perspective, allowing you to set things right. Upon making situations right in your life, you can then love your neighbors as yourself by extending these benefits to others through your thoughts, feelings, emotions, words, and actions, thereby spreading the force of love that comes from God.

Jesus Christ's death demonstrates God's love for humanity. It provides a guideline where we learn that love is sacrificing your ability to blame, hate, hold grudges, take revenge, be malicious, scornful, and unkind in thoughts, words, and deeds, and instead forgive ourselves and others. By others, I mean anyone who has caused you hurt and harm or whom you hold accountable for your life being the way it is.

Forgiveness is freeing and life-giving; unforgiveness blocks the flow of God's love. If you do not receive God's love for yourself, you stop your connection with God. Likewise, if you receive God's love for yourself but do not share it with others, you create a blockage in transmuting love between yourself and others. The blockage between yourself and others inevitably causes resistance in your ability to progress in your purpose.

Galatians 5:6 says, "For, in Christ Jesus, neither circumcision nor uncircumcision has any value. The only thing that counts is faith expressing itself through love." Regardless of who you are, the pain or injustice you've endured, regardless of your innocence or your role in your pain, you should endeavor to forgive, for there is a purpose in your pain. If you refuse to forgive, you will create a blockage for yourself. This blockage will prevent you from cultivating understanding and pursuing your purpose. Love is akin to forgiveness. Unless you forgive, you will never rise higher in your ability to love.

Scriptural Affirmation

- I have an advocate who helps me and is with me forever. John 14:16.
- My transgressions are blotted out. My sins are forgotten forever. Isaiah 43:25.
- God is merciful towards me. He forgets all of my sins. Hebrews 8:12 and 10:17.
- I am the temple of God. God's Spirit dwells within me. 1 Corinthians 3:16.
- My God is faithful. He will not let me be tempted beyond what I can bear. He will make a way so I can endure temptation. 1 Corinthians 10:13.
- God loves me so much that He gave His only son, the full manifestation of Love, as a sacrifice for my sin so I can be free. John 3:16.
- I stand without guilt before God. 1 John 3:20.
- My love comes from God, and with God's love, I love others. John 4:7.
- I forgive others so that I also can be forgiven by God. Matthew 6:14.
- I release all judgment and condemnation. I forgive so that I may be forgiven. Luke 6:37.
- My God is forgiving and good. He abounds in love for all who call to Him. Psalms 86:5.
- With the measure of love I have for myself, I give unto others. Leviticus 19:17-18 & Matthew 22:39.

3

THE PURPOSE IN YOUR PAIN-CALLING

Joseph was the eleventh of twelve sons and the most loved child of Jacob. His father loved him so much that he made a particular coat for him of many colors. Unfortunately, Jacob's love for Joseph made the other sons very jealous. To make matters worse, Joseph had a dream and shared with his family that they would all bow before him.

As a young boy whom his brothers already disliked, the dream made them more furious towards him; even Jacob rebuked Joseph for such a dream. Nevertheless, the dream was from God, and it communicated that Joseph was indeed going to be a leader to whom they all would bow before. God, in that dream, shared a glimpse of Joseph's purpose and destiny with Joseph.

The fury in the brothers caused them to conspire to kill Joseph. However, one brother suggested instead that they throw Joseph into a cistern. After throwing Joseph into the cistern, another brother suggested they sell him to the Ishmaelite merchants who happened to be passing by. Instead, they pulled Joseph from the cistern and sold him for twenty shekels of silver (approximately five dollars and forty-eight cents United States dollars). The brothers subsequently killed a goat, covered Joseph's coat in its blood, and brought it back home to their father, Jacob, to report that ferocious animals allegedly killed Joseph. The news broke their father's heart.

Joseph was brought to Egypt and sold to Potiphar, one of Pharaoh's officials and the captain of the guard. The Lord was with Joseph, and Joseph humbly served, so much so that he was responsible for Potiphar's entire household. In everything Joseph did, he prospered, and Joseph remained faithful to God.

While performing his duties, Potiphar's wife tried to seduce Joseph to sleep with her. When he resisted, she lied, which caused Joseph to be imprisoned. While in prison, Joseph used his gifts to help others. He remained humble, faithful, and committed to the vision God gave Him in the dream and the purpose for which God created Him.

After some years had passed, Joseph was inspired by God with the interpretation of a dream that Pharaoh had. Having interpreted the dream, Joseph was released from prison and assigned responsibility over all the land of Egypt. With his promotion, Joseph was given much privilege and prestige. Pharaoh's dream suggested a season of abundance and famine, and Joseph was responsible for navigating both seasons to ensure food supply for all was sufficient.

It so happened that Joseph's family was also affected by the famine, and they had to come to Egypt to obtain food for their father's household.

When they came to Egypt, they did not recognize Joseph, their brother, whom they had taken advantage of and left to die, but Joseph recognized them. Joseph could have taken revenge for all that His brothers did to him. He could have held a grudge, and he could have prevented them from receiving food. He could have hated them. With Joseph's status and power in Egypt, he could have had them executed. Instead, with a simple change in his perception, Joseph showed that he was awakened to the power of love and that love could transmute pain into purpose. Joseph realized the miracle in his pain. God used Joseph's experiences of sufferings to transport him into a position of purpose, where He would recognize the dream he had when he was just a young boy. His miracle was having a different perspective on his painful experiences because he trusted God's promise to him in his childhood dream.

If Joseph had not gone through all his sufferings, he would not be able to help the nation as they navigated the years of famine, he would not have been able to provide his family with food, and God would not have used him to move the children of Israel into alignment with His plans for redemption. Instead, through Joseph's pain, God could perform His purpose for humanity.

Just as Joseph realized the miracle and purpose in his pain, there is also a miracle and purpose in your pain for you to discover.

Jeremiah 1:5 states, "Before I formed you in the womb, I knew you; before you were born, I set you apart; I appointed you as a prophet to the nations." This tells you that God has a plan for you. Your life is preordained. With your mission established, you came to this earth with everything you need to succeed. Whatever you experienced or are experiencing, God had already known. Some of you were aware of God's plan for your life when you were young. You may have had a dream, a random thought that resonates deeply, or even an idea that may look impossible, but you cannot shake it out of your mind. Others do not know how to clarify their purpose amidst life's turmoil and confusion.

Life is set up so that your experiences are the tools that will cause you to become aware of your purpose. Though some of your experiences may be pleasant and give you "aha" moments as a sign of confirmation of your purpose, it is often the most unpleasant experiences that cause you to realize your purpose. God will not call you to a purpose for which you do not have experience. Like grapes are crushed before the wine is produced, you will be destroyed before you are qualified. Like olives are pressed and kneaded before the oil can be extracted, you will be pressed and kneaded before you are fit. You cannot serve a purpose effectively in an area you have no experience in or have not overcome. You can only be to others what you are to yourself. Therefore, "Do not be surprised at the fiery ordeal that has come on you to test you, as though something strange was happening to you. But rejoice since you participate in the sufferings of Christ, so that you may be overjoyed when his glory is revealed." (1Peter 4:12-13).

Painful experiences are not uncommon. Many people may experience the same pain; however, for every individual, a unique ingredient creates a miracle that will guide them to fulfilling their purpose. The unique element may be your age, your location, your vocation, your gender, your parents, or your nationality, or it can very well be a particular year or season. God is multidimensional, and likewise, His purpose for your life. You are not limited in your cause.

You must be ready and willing to accept the Call of God to create this shift in your life. You must be willing to face the fear of opening up to and acknowledging your pain, take responsibility for the direction of your future, and know that the purpose of God for your life is yours to realize and navigate to fulfillment. I am not by any means suggesting that this is an easy process. It takes time to convert your pain into lessons for yourself, and it will take courage to share them with others. However, with this knowledge, you can, by faith, shift your life into a positive, purposeful, and fulfilling direction guided fully by the Holy Spirit.

Scriptural Affirmations

- Because Christ forgave me, I forgive those who have harmed me. Ephesians 4:32.
- My trials and temptations are for perfecting and completing myself. James 1:2-4.
- I am called according to God's purposes. All things work together for my good. Romans 8:28.
- My suffering is temporary. After it has ended, God shall restore me and make me strong, firm, and steadfast. 1 Peter 5:10.
- I shall perceive and fulfill the purpose for my pain. My pain shall not be wasted. Hebrews 11:1.
- The Lord refreshes my soul and guides me along the right paths for His name's sake. Psalms 23:3.
- Every experience in my life was pre-ordained for a Godly purpose. With God, I have victory. Jeremiah 29:11.
- As I participate in the suffering of Christ, I am assured of joy when His glory is revealed. 1 Peter 4:13.
- My Lord prepares a table before me in the presence of my enemies. My head is anointed, and my cup overflows. Psalms 23:5.
- For this reason, I was born. John 18:37.
- I am chosen. I am royalty. I am of a Holy Nation. I am God's special possession. I stand in the beautiful light of Christ. My life is a profession of praise to Jesus Christ. 1 Peter 2:9.
- My present suffering cannot be compared with the glory that will be revealed in me. Romans 8:18.

PART TWO

THE CALL AND THE CALLER

*The thief comes only to steal, kill, and destroy; I have come
that they may have life and have it to the full.*
John 10:10.

4

DISCOVERING THE CALL

Among the definitions of the Merriam-Webster Online Dictionary, the word "call" means:

- To speak/utter in a loud, distinct voice.
- To announce/read loudly and authoritatively.
- To command or request to come or be present.
- To summon to a particular activity, employment, or office.
- To invite or command to meet,

The definitions allude to changing one's focus, state, position, and or attention from one thing to another in a way that suggests leaping forward, and it speaks with urgency and importance.

The Lord called Abram in Genesis 12:1-4. He told Abram, "Go from your country, your people, and your father's household to the land I will show you." Abram obeyed the Lord and departed as the Lord had spoken to him. Moses was tending his father-in-law's flock when the Lord called Him. The Lord said, "So now, go. I am sending you to Pharoah to bring my people, the Israelites, out of Egypt" (Exodus 3:10). Moses obeyed by asking his father-in-law for release to follow the Lord. Samuel was called by name four times by the Lord. At the fourth call, the Lord called, "Samuel! Samuel!" and Samuel responded obediently by saying, "Speak, for your servant is listening" (1 Samuel 3:10). Through Samuel's obedience, the Lord told Samuel the purpose for which He called him. In the New Testament, Jesus saw Matthew, the

Tax collector, sitting at the tax office. Jesus instructed Matthew to "follow me" (Matthew 9:9). Matthew arose and followed Jesus.

In Matthew 4:18-22, Jesus said to brothers Peter and Andrew, "Come, follow me." They responded by immediately leaving their nets behind and following Jesus. They were at work, on the sea, for they were fishers. Jesus called them and gave them purpose. Jesus went further and saw two more brothers, James and John. They were mending nets with their father. He called them, and like Peter and Andrew, they immediately left their father and the boat to follow Jesus. In John 1:43, Jesus said to Phillip, "follow Me." Phillip not only followed Jesus, but he also did what Jesus was doing. Phillip called Nathaniel and shared the promised Messiah's good news.

Nathaniel also responded to the call and met Jesus, whom he followed. In Luke 19:1-10 Jesus called Zacchaeus, a chief tax collector, "come down immediately. I must stay at your house today." Zacchaeus came down at once. Jesus commanded the man with infirmity at the Pool of Bethesda, "Get up! Pick up your mat and walk (John 5:8). Immediately, the man was well, got up, and walked. In John 11:38-44, Jesus went to the tomb where His friend Lazarus lay dead for four days and said, "Lazarus, come out!" (John 11:43). With Jesus' command, Lazarus came out of the tomb at once.

The calls were straightforward; those called moved at once and followed Jesus' command. While some summoned were told their purpose, they had no clue where the journey would lead. The key, however, is that they believed in Jesus Christ the Caller, rose from the state they were in, and obediently followed the instructions He gave along their journey.

In the same way, Jesus calls you to follow Him. He said, "Here I am! I stand at the door and knock. If anyone hears My voice and opens the door, I will come in and eat with that person, and they with me" (Revelations 3:20). "Eat" as used in this verse is used as a reference for fellowship. Therefore, if you respond to the call of God, the Holy Spirit will enter your heart and restore you through fellowship with Jesus Christ. Through this fellowship, your purpose will be revealed to you, and like Nathaniel, who believed in Jesus Christ, you will see and do greater things (John1:51). When you believe and trust God, you will be empowered through the Holy Spirit to do greater things than Jesus did while He was on earth (John 14:12).

The Call, therefore, is a divine command from God, through the power of The Holy Spirit, to shift from your current state, mentally and otherwise, possibly forsaking all things and people you held in high esteem and move forward for your greater divine good and Godly purpose.

Unlike natural journeys that depend on worldly logic and experience, the call is a sacred journey where help and guidance are received from the bible and through the instructions of the Holy Spirit. Where God leads, He protects and provides.

Scripture Affirmations

- I consider and fix my mind upon Jesus Christ, the hope of my heavenly calling. Hebrews 3:1.
- God chooses me for Himself before the foundations of the world. I am purposely adopted through Jesus Christ to the praise of His glorious name. Ephesians 1:4-5.
- I belong to Jesus Christ by His calling. Romans 1:6.
- By answering the call of Jesus Christ, I am saved. I have come to the knowledge of the truth. 1 Timothy 2:4.
- I am a new creation. I look with great expectancy in Jesus Christ to all things new. 2 Corinthians 5:17-20.
- Great and more extraordinary things shall I do, for I believe in Jesus Christ and have answered His call. John 14:12.
- I am God's creation. I was created in Jesus Christ for good works. My work was prepared for me ahead of time so that I could walk in them. Ephesians 2:10.
- My face is radiant with joy because I look to Him. I shall never be ashamed. Psalms 34:5.
- I have confidence in Jesus Christ because I seek His wisdom first. I completely trust God. Matthew 6:33-34.
- Having publicly accepted the call of Jesus Christ, I surrender everything that will hinder me. With endurance, I take on the journey that lies before me with my eyes fixed entirely on Jesus, the source and perfector of my faith. Hebrews 12:1-2.
- I proclaim the praises of the one who called me out of darkness into His marvelous light. I am of the family of God, and I receive His mercy. 1 Peter 2:9-10.
- I honor Jesus Christ as the Lord of my heart. I will respectfully defend the hope within me to keep my conscience clear and shame all who denounce my Christian life. 1 Peter 3:15-16.

5

WHY ARE YOU CALLED?

When a visionary decides to bring his ideas for creating a business to fruition, his first action is to choose partners who will assist with the planning and execution of his ideas. The partners he solicits are people who believe in his vision and share similar values for the business. These partners come together as the foundation of the company and are strategically assigned responsibilities that will aid in shaping the direction of the business. Others are called to function in different capacities as the project comes together. Understanding this strategy has given me insight into the verse in Matthew 22:14 "For many are invited, but few are chosen." God knows that his creation plans required people strategically chosen to build his team. The chosen ones are the foundation on which humanity and other things on earth would be shaped and developed. God decided to create a few people with character and integrity who believe in His vision of creation and the salvation of people to execute His plans. These chosen people seemed to have been born out of the womb knowing and committed to their purpose and spent their life pursuing it successfully and absolutely nothing else. Having had the chosen ones appointed, Jesus knew He would need others to work in various areas to aid in the awareness, growth, development, care, and maintenance of humanity and the rest of creation, according to His will and desires. He, therefore, invited many others by creating situations that would allow them to choose if they should accept the call to rise to specific roles and duties that would lead them to fulfill their purpose and help shape life on Earth. These individuals had the opportunity to partner with God in spreading love and advancing life by creating and leaving legacies behind in the Universe.

In Matthew 22:1-10, we read of a parable Jesus shared about a wedding feast. It is told of a King who arranged a marriage for his son and sent out his servants to call those invited to the wedding. The wedding was fully organized and ready to receive the guests, but they were unwilling to come. They ignored, refused, violently opposed the invitation, and continued their business. The King was displeased. He expelled and destroyed those who rejected his call and were deemed unworthy. The king then called all other people willing to attend the wedding, good people and bad people, and with this invitation, the wedding feast was filled with guests. When the king came to see the guests that accepted the invitation, one guest was present but not dressed for the wedding. The man was speechless when asked why he was present with no wedding garments on. The king ordered the man to be bound up, hands and feet, and thrown out into utter darkness where there would be weeping and gnashing of teeth.

Jesus Christ has a specific purpose for which He calls each of us. He calls us to fulfill His vision in this world, which is why he made us in His image and likeness, and, like the king, He made careful preparations for us to serve our purpose. In the time between birth and His call, we gain experiences, some good and some bad, and we are expected to prepare ourselves through these experiences. Take a moment to imagine everything that happens in the world, your country, your community, your home, and something that has happened directly to you and the people around you since your birth and this current moment.

You will see this; as you enjoy the world advancing in science, medicine, technology, engineering, art, music, mathematics, and social and religious knowledge, you find that the state of morality and security erodes the fibers of life. Relationships are being destroyed. Family, as we know from creation, is changing drastically and dramatically. Money is valued more than humanity. Food to support the health and sustenance of life is being genetically modified, making it less healthy for consumption.

Sickness and diseases are rampant and detrimental, and while healthcare is accessible, only some social groups seem to have proper access. Wealth is controlled, and only a few are willing or able to access it. There are racial, religious, and political wars in some regions. People are scared to exist because of the color of their skin. Cultures, traditions, and norms are changing and confusing many. People's rights to personal choice are being scorned. There are some individuals suffering from various types of neglect and abuse. Poverty is increasing, and more people live in despair, desperation, and depression. So many are suffering, and this was not the intention of Jesus Christ when He created humanity. Discernment is reduced in congregations. The church has become complacent where, as the representation of God's family, they seemingly compete with society's structure and morals. The different names of God are removed from conversations and public spaces, and to some people, God's existence seems vague and ambiguous.

While there are so many secrets in this world to uncover, there are still so many people with skills, talents, abilities, solutions, and creative ideas locked inside them who need to discover the creator, Jesus Christ, and His vision and purpose for their life. Therefore, if any of the conditions listed above, or any other that you can think of, have affected you, robbed you, or made you angry or concerned, it could be an intrinsic lead to your purpose. You may have a role to play in fixing these issues. These issues are a means to propel you into action to create change. The problem is that you can only make a lasting change if you are empowered and directed by the Holy Spirit. If you accept the call and refuse to prepare for your purpose, you will be like the guest who showed up at the wedding wearing no wedding garments.

You are called to come to Jesus Christ to be restored in Him and to receive His Spirit. Jesus Christ desires to help you become more knowledgeable about who He is. He wants you to know who you are in Him. He wants to give you His vision of whom you can become so you can participate in His creative and redemptive work. Jesus's call is to surrender all you are and do and allow Him to give you a new perspective on the life you are here on earth to live. His call is a priority, it is primary, and it is of utmost importance in life. Surrender yourself to

His will and let His will make you great. There is plenty of work He desires for you to do, and He wants you to do it to the degree you are experienced and prepared. Surrender yourself to His will and let His will make you great.

Scriptural Affirmations

- I am an offspring of Jesus Christ. In Him I live, I move and exist. Acts 17:28.
- I am His workmanship, created in His image and according to His likeness, for works, He had prepared before I could walk in them. Ephesians 2:10.
- I have a predestined inheritance in Him according to His will and purpose. Ephesians 1:11.
- God's word is correct, and His work is trustworthy. Psalm 33:4.
- I am made in His image and according to His likeness, and I have dominion over all His creations. Genesis 1:26.
- I am called to follow Jesus Christ's example, to partake in His sufferings, to do good and endure so that I can bring favor with God. 1 Peter 2:20-21.
- Jesus Christ is the author of life; He existed from the beginning and knows everything concerning me. John 1:1-3.
- Being in Christ, I reap according to my efforts. 2 Thessalonians 3:10.
- I shall speak up for those who have no voice. I shall seek justice for all who are dispossessed. I shall make wise judgments and defend the cause of the oppressed and needy. Proverbs 31:8-9.
- I shall denounce all evils and be cleansed. I shall do what is good. I shall seek justice and correct the oppressor. My work shall defend the rights of the fatherless and the widows. Isaiah 1:16-17.
- The Lord knows what is good for me and what He requires of me. I shall act justly, love faithfulness, and walk humbly with God. Micah 6:8.

> - As a manager of the various grace of God, I shall use the gifts the Lord has given me to serve others. I shall speak God's word and serve God with the strength He provides. The Lord shall be glorified in everything I do. 1 Peter 4:10-11.

28

6

LEARNING THE TYPES OF CALLING

There are four critical stages every human being is called to experience during their lifetime on earth. First, there is the call to enter this earthly realm through birth. Second, there is a call from the Holy Spirit to be reconciled with God through salvation. Third, after salvation, we are called to partner with the Holy Spirit through Jesus Christ to spread Love and participate in the redemptive work of creation. This call is the call to purpose. Finally, we are called to transition from our work and time on earth through the experience of death.

Based on my biblical knowledge, God created, ordained, and sent human beings into this world, and we are also appointed to die. Because of the specific purpose attached to our lives, we are called to experience situations that will help to drive us closer to God so He can reveal his intention to us. If we refuse and rebel against drawing closer to God, we cheat ourselves out of abundant life. The consequence of a life without Jesus Christ is a life without meaning, purpose, and value. It is characterized by living miserably, being confused, and lacking importance, impact, influence, and peace in our life and environment. Some individuals numb themselves until their appointed time of death, while others choose to take their own lives and end their journey prematurely. This leads me to believe that of the four types of calls. God gives every human being the opportunity of free will to choose the two calls that will determine how their life on earth will be spent and how life in eternity will be after death. These two calls are the call to salvation and the call to purpose.

The Call to Salvation

The call to salvation is Jesus Christ's official invitation to you to participate in His redemptive work in the world. This invitation requires you to make the most crucial choice in your life, for it is through salvation that you are restored to Him, your Creator, and the purpose for which you were born. This means that after accepting the call to salvation, you cannot continue pursuing God and your life through your will and intellect. God intentionally requires you to be restored so you can follow Him through His wisdom and will for your life.

Being restored to Jesus Christ is a process. The Apostle Paul urges that you "offer your bodies as a living sacrifice, holy and pleasing to God; this is your true and proper worship. Do not conform to the pattern of this world, but be transformed by renewing your mind. Then you will be able to test and approve what God's will is; His good, pleasing and perfect will" (Romans 12:1-2). Also, Mark 2:22 states, "And no one pours new wine into old wineskins. Otherwise, the wine will burst the skins, and both the wine and the wineskins will be ruined. No, they pour new wine into new wineskins."

When you answer the call of Salvation, you must resolve to leave behind your perception of your old self, fears, worries, beliefs, and shame, among other limitations, and be wholly dedicated to a transformation journey. For human beings, the most effective way to transform, as purported by the scripture, is to begin from within by renewing your mind. Renewing your mind starts with knowing the God who calls you. He said, "Here I am! I stand at the door and knock. If anyone hears my voice and opens the door, I will come in and eat with that person, and they with me" Revelations 3:20.

Jesus Christ is eager to fellowship with you so you can know His thoughts and plans for your life. In John 1:1-4 it is written, "In the beginning was the Word, and the Word was with God, and the Word was God. He was with God in the beginning. Through Him, all things were made; without Him, nothing was made that has been made. In Him was life, and that life was the light of all humanity." In the English language, the term *word* is the symbol used for vocalized thoughts. The word thought comes from the Old English word "*þoht geþoht,*" which means the process of thinking. The word *think*, as in action thinking, stems from the word "*þencan*" which means to conceive in mind or to consider. This means, in the beginning, was God's thoughts, and with His thoughts, all things were made; without His thoughts, nothing was made that has been made. In God's thoughts was life, and that life was the light of all humanity. It also means that you were conceived in the mind of God. He considers you, which explains why "the Word became flesh and made His dwelling among us (humanity)" (John1:14). This verse reveals the presence of God's son Jesus Christ who came into the world as a witness of the truth and love of God, to teach and preach of the kingdom of heaven, to call sinners to repentance, and to restore humanity to holiness by giving his life as a ransom for our sins. Even in His death, Jesus Christ still had you in His mind.

John 14:15-21 states, "If you love me, keep my commands, and I will ask the Father, and he will give you another advocate to help you and be with you forever- the Spirit of truth. The world cannot accept him because it neither sees nor knows him. But you know him; he lives with you and will be in you. I will not leave you as orphans; I will come to you. Before long, the world will not see me anymore, but you will see me. Because I live, you also will live. On that day, you will realize that I am in my Father, and you are in me, and I am in you. Whoever has my commands and keeps them is the one who loves me. My Father will love the one who loves me, and I will love them and show myself to them." This tells you that the Holy Spirit is God's Word within you. The Holy Spirit speaks through you and allows you to create. Jesus Christ is always talking to your heart so you can know Him and let Him guide you into transformation. Through you, the Holy Spirit transforms formlessness to form, nothingness into something, confusion into clarity, ashes into beauty, fear into strength, pain into purpose, mourning into gladness, and your sorrow into joy. The Word is powerful. "For the Word of God is alive and active. Sharper than any double-edged sword, it penetrates even to dividing soul and spirit, joints and marrow; it judges the thoughts and attitudes of the heart. Nothing in all creation is hidden from God's sight. Everything is uncovered and laid bare before his eyes to whom we must give account." Hebrews 4:12-13. God knows you. God knows every fiber of your being. God has you in His mind and consideration, and He calls you to enter into the process of getting aligned with the knowledge He has of you. This process usually unfolds in four stages.

The first stage is learning your identity in God. You were made in the image and likeness of God upon being born into this world. But, unfortunately, you were also born in sin and shaped in iniquity (Psalms 51:5). All you have learned about life, your decisions, and your actions are from your interactions with the sinful world you live in. By accepting the call of salvation, you receive His Spirit, the Holy Spirit. The Holy Spirit is your helper, comforter, advocate, counselor, and intercessor. The Holy Spirit transforms your mind into the mind of God, allowing you to become aligned with God and His knowledge and purpose for your life. Knowing this, you will value yourself with the same value God has placed on you. You will learn, make decisions and take actions based on what the Holy Spirit communicates to you for the rest of your life.

Your acceptance of salvation automatically changes your identity in God. You become the righteousness of God in Christ Jesus. You are saved and forgiven. You are a saint because of your faith in Jesus Christ. You become His workmanship, a ready and available vessel for God to pour His values and desires into. Once you obey God, all His promises will be yours (Reference Deuteronomy 28:1-14). As the scripture states, "The LORD will make you the head, not the tail. If you pay attention to the commands of the LORD your God that I give you this day and carefully follow them, you will always be at the top, never at the bottom", Deuteronomy 28:13. Your new identity allows you to stand above all your fears and limitations. Your new identity affirms that your truth and value are in God.

Your next step is a relationship. Your identity in God is reinforced through a relationship with the Holy Spirit. Your relationship must include prayer, reading the bible, meditating, fasting, professing your faith, and having fellowship with other believers.

Praying is communicating with God, which must be done as often and consistently as possible. Praying helps you to align with God's will for your life. When you pray, you tell God your heart, and He provides comfort, answers, and directions. By trusting God's response, you strengthen your audience with the Holy Spirit so you can become more like Jesus, experience miracles, and avoid temptations.

Along with prayer, you must read your bible. The Bible is the living word of God. It contains the historical events of creation and the revelation of God to His people. The Bible tells you about God's nature and encourages you as you journey with the Holy Spirit into fulfilling your purpose and life on earth. As you read and learn scriptures and the mind of God, you should learn to meditate. Through meditation, you get still and quiet before God by taking your attention off yourself and your needs and wants and allowing God to communicate and fellowship with you and show Himself real.

Fasting is vital in strengthening your relationship with God through the Holy Spirit. Fasting is an intentional act of abstaining from food and sometimes drinks. Fasting allows you to seek God through prayer to gain discipline, power, wisdom, and understanding regarding complex and uncertain experiences or occurrences.

As your relationship strengthens, you begin to profess your faith in God. You'll get excited and want to adore your new lover, the Lord Jesus Christ. You begin to sing songs of praise and say words of adoration and affirmations to Him. You'll want to spend more time with the Lord as you learn, grow, and see that everything you do reflects your love for Him.

The second stage is learning your identity in this world. You were given a body to dwell in when born into this world. Your body is God's temple and physical representation on earth. It is the home of your spirit and the workshop for developing the essence of who you are and what you will do in this world. Through your body, you can express the gifts, skills, talents, abilities, eccentricities, and quirks you came into this world with. Through your body, you will have encounters and experiences that will impact you to influence your purpose.

It is important to know that you are not your body but a spirit dwelling in your body. Before Christ, you had a sin-natured spirit that led you to do many things not of God. Upon accepting Christ, that sin-natured spirit was replaced with the righteous Spirit of God. This means that before Christ, your body was under the directives of your sinful nature; your actions, behaviors, and practices were influenced by sin. Upon accepting Christ, the orders changed. As such, you must actively and intentionally change to align with your new moral nature.

When you were born, you were given a family. Your family plays a fundamental role in your socialization and upbringing. It is in your family that you should receive and feel unconditional love. It is in your family that you are to learn to love other individuals. Your family is where you are expected to obtain security, protection, guidance, advice, and support. You may not have been given any physical, emotional, or psychological support from your family; you were probably abused, abandoned, or given up for adoption. But, it was all part of the process that contributed towards your purpose. God is unchanging yet dynamic in His nature. He did not create you to be defined or limited by your circumstances. Instead, He created you to be empowered by them.

The location and conditions you were born into or experienced as a child helped develop your perceptions of the world. That, along with your interaction with your family, helps mold and influence your purpose in the world and causes you to develop values, principles, and ethics with which you lived your life before getting saved.

Up to the point of you reading this book, you have gained experiences and exposure. Experiences and exposures give you lessons and develop your abilities. The lessons determine what you like and dislike and cause you to develop various weaknesses and fears. They help with developing your hopes, dreams, and desires. The experiences and exposures have also caused you to have particular thought patterns, goals, and plans.

Some of your experiences and exposures may be very cruel and unpleasant. Salvation is the first and best step to getting healed. Prayer and deliverance services are also helpful for healing. In many cases, however, salvation, prayer, and deliverance alone will not help you to overcome some of the cruel and unpleasant experiences you've had. As the medical doctor exists as a resource to help improve your physical health, there are trained professional counselors and therapists to help you with your mental health and overall well-being. Therapy is powerful. Utilize the resources available to get the best out of your life experiences because all you are is important to your calling and purpose. Learning your identity in God, accepting your identity in the world, receiving forgiveness from God, forgiving those who have wronged you, and embracing a continuous healing journey is the only way to experience positive transformation.

As you heal, accept your identity, and take the necessary steps to achieve transformation, you should identify and establish your list of core values to live your new life. Your core values are words used to describe how you want to be seen, perceived, and treated by everyone you come in contact with. Since you are now a believer and desire to be seen and treated as such, your core values must be based on biblical ethics and characteristics to align with God's nature and will.

As you walk in your newness, you will be inspired by the Holy Spirit with desires and goals. Some may be of old that you had forgotten or thought was impossible, and some may be new desires. In your prayers, put your desires before God. In all your doings, "Take delight in the Lord, and He will give you the desires of your heart" (Psalms 37:4).

After identifying and establishing your values and goals, your next step is creating boundaries you will live by. Your boundaries are the standards, principles, and norms you will develop to separate the old you from the new you in your physical realm. Your boundaries should communicate your needs, wants, desires, feelings, and actions you deem acceptable. As an individual in the transformation process, your boundaries should express how you treat yourself and the treatment you expect others to give you. Your boundaries will reinforce your self-respect, self-esteem, and self-value.

When God created you, He looked at you and said you are good. Nothing you have been through can change that. You will greatly appreciate your uniqueness and identity when you learn to accept and believe this about yourself. You will place a high value on yourself as you integrate your transformed self into the world, the third stage in accepting the call to Salvation.

Integrating yourself as a transformed individual is a form of rebirth or re-emergence. This process will require you to apply your knowledge of your identity in Christ and your identity in this world through your vision, values, priorities, and goals. You should make all your decisions and act according to your core values. For example, your friendships must be chosen through your core values. You should determine your deportment and choice of entertainment for pleasure through your core values. Your communication styles and other interests, including social media platforms, must be chosen, constructed, and tailored to your values. Most importantly, your love interests and chosen person for marriage must be decided upon through your values, vision, and what you consider to be your priorities.

Integrating yourself as a transformed individual should also involve taking the lessons from the different stories in the bible and applying them to the different areas of life, such as love, relationships, family, finance, accountability, health, leadership, and other places where you may gain more experiences. As you interact with others, you should also be flexible enough to refine or change values that do not give you the most efficient results in pursuing your goals and vision. Life is not perfect. You will fail sometimes. You will make plans, and they don't go accordingly. But seek to learn the lessons in all your failures, and don't get stuck on temporal successes. As you do your part to align with God's will for your life, ensure that your image of yourself aligns with your character so you can develop integrity among others.

Finally, in the fourth stage, you embrace your growth while preparing for greater empowerment. As you deepen your relationship with the Holy Spirit, you will become more comfortable talking to God. You will find that The Holy Spirit will begin to trust you more with His wisdom and knowledge and continuously deposit information into your spirit. What the Holy Spirit will start to do is to test you. Tests are necessary to pull out areas within your soul that need to change and grow.

You will be in various conflicts through your integrated interaction with the world. These will be between you and other people, your health, finances, or your community. The lessons and consequences you will experience will be life-changing. They may involve ending a marriage or a relationship that is out of alignment with God's will for your life. You will be required to cut off some friendships that are not contributing to the new vision God has communicated to you. You may have to relocate to a new home address or leave your job or career. You may have to withdraw from some projects you've spent years building or choose a lifestyle lesser than the one you were leading. These conflicts are to teach you more about yourself and the world you live in and direct you in ways that will influence your growth in God and as an individual. For God to do something new through you, He has to do something new to you.

As you go through this stage, people will misunderstand, ridicule, and talk badly about you. You may have to make choices and do things that make you look ridiculous. Growth is an ugly, painful, uncertain, confusing, challenging, and lonely process that must be endured. It teaches you to be humble, disciplined, and courageous. Most of all, it teaches you to depend on God.

When you are grown, you begin to bloom; you will bear the beautiful qualities known as the fruits of the spirit. These are love, joy, peace, forbearance, kindness, goodness, faithfulness, gentleness, and self-control (Galatians 5:22-23). The Word of God advises that you are known as a child of God by the fruits you bear.

During this time, you would have been inspired with desires from the Holy Spirit and received urges to serve in areas that align with your gifts, talents, skills, and abilities. You should volunteer your time, energy, and resources. It would be best if you were willing to say yes to opportunities that come your way, especially those that appeal to your desires and align with your values. When serving in those areas, you are investing in building yourself as you are serving others to the honor and glory of God. Whatever you do should fill you with inspiration and gratification, so you want to do more for others, thereby developing your passion for service. Anything outside of that will drain you and cause burnout and loss of interest and commitment.

The more you serve, the more you should seek to learn about the vocations you are passionate about. Look to others ahead of you in said vocation for inspiration, mentorship, and coaching. Learn the requisite characteristics that will make you more effective in service. Seek to emulate healthy qualities, habits, and attributes you admire and believe will bring you to the next level. It is a cheat code to be more effective in a more efficient time.

Your service to God is not limited to the church's program. You may be called to serve outside of the church. Your service to God is your vocation. While your vocation may allow you a salary in many instances, this is not always the case. You may also need to have a job. Whatever your job is, ensure that it aligns with your values and vision so it does not prevent you from serving God.

Finally, though Paul encourages us never to forsake the gathering of saints, he also states that He is all things to all men so some may be saved. We live in a big world, and people are everywhere. God desires us to reach everyone through our ministry and purpose. Whatever you do, ensure that you do it to serve others as a ministry for God that the Holy Spirit guides. Ensure you stay connected to a fellowship so you can always "come home" to your family in God for fellowship, encouragement, brotherly or sisterly love, connection, and strength.

As you serve, never become complacent. Instead, remain prayerful, mindful, and watchful for the moments requiring you to shift into your divine elevation.

The Call to Purpose

As you are satisfied with serving in your calling and fulfilling your various potentials, God has a way of calling you into a higher realm. This is the call to your purpose.

The call to purpose is crucial because it requires you to make a tremendous sacrifice to evolve into the version of yourself that is effective for the realm in which you are called to operate. The call to purpose usually comes when you least expect it. It comes with more significant responsibilities than you can fathom and requires greater power than your human abilities. The call to purpose requires courage!

There is a story about a rich young ruler in Luke 18:18-25 who wanted to inherit eternal life. He had kept all the commandments since he was a boy. You would call him a faithful servant who did right by God; however, Jesus advised the rich young ruler that he still lacked one thing. Jesus said, "Sell everything you have and give to the poor, and you will have treasure in heaven. Then come follow me". (verse 22). The rich young ruler became sad because he was wealthy and did not see himself giving up his wealth for uncertainty. This, however, is the requirement when you are called into your purpose.

The call to purpose presents itself so that you may have to walk away from the life you have built and established for yourself; the job, the vocation, the church, or the community you love. You may have made many changes and decided to settle, only to realize that God is calling you to do more. The changes you will be required to undergo will cause you to question yourself, God, and even the existence you spent time, resources, and energy building. This call will not make sense to you in the beginning.

The call usually comes to you in the form of a word from God, an unexpected opportunity, or a sudden change in your life circumstances that leave you no choice but to be desperate to become what God wants you to be. While the call to purpose may not make sense to you, your response to the call to purpose will distinguish between your pride in your accomplishments and comfort zones and your trust in God's requirements.

The call to purpose is to evolve and leap into greatness. The call to purpose is your next-level shift. The call to purpose is when all your experiences, the exposures you've had, and your passion unite to step into the transformative move of God in the universe. Your purpose is the divine moment when the Holy Spirit orchestrates a supernatural transference or deposit of His power within you to enter the flow of His sacred work on this earth.

The call to purpose will unearth why you went through everything in your past. It will give you meaning and explain why everything you did to transform yourself was necessary. It will explain why choosing the right partner, creating the right family, and having the right friendships are crucial because purpose requires your entire lifestyle to be in one accord.

Your purpose is both challenging and rewarding. It will stretch you while filling you with gratitude, joy, and bliss. Your purpose is not about you; it is about God through the power of the Holy Spirit, working through you in this earthly realm to help His people to be saved, restored, renewed, comforted, provided for, protected, healed, have knowledge of Him, and empowered through as many mediums as He allows.

Your purpose will cause you to come alive with greater light, energy, and intensity of passion. The power of desire is likened to the love of God. It ignites and creates energy. Energy is magnetic, which attracts and transfers.

When you are operating in your purpose, you do not have to cajole, coerce, instigate, or manipulate anyone through the use of fear to follow you, collaborate with you, or contribute to your work. The right people, those you are to serve and those to invest in your cause, are naturally drawn to you. This is what the scriptures mean in Matthew 5:14-16, "You are the light of the world. A town built on a hill cannot be hidden. Neither do people light a lamp and put it under a bowl. Instead, they put it on its stand, and it gives light to everyone in the house. In the same way, let your light shine before others, that they may see your good deeds and glorify your Father in heaven."

Scriptural Affirmations

- I am God's handiwork. I am created in Christ Jesus and predestined by God to do good works. Ephesian 2:10.
- By the divine power of Jesus Christ and the knowledge of His glory and goodness, I have everything I need to live a Godly life. 2 Peter 1:3.
- Every ounce of my being is created by God while in my mother's womb. Psalms 139:13.
- I shall praise God because He made me fearfully and wonderfully. Nothing about me was hidden. Psalms 139:14.
- I am grateful for the days of my small beginnings. They are the strong foundation for my extraordinary and purposeful life. Zechariah 4:10.
- God has raised me for this very purpose, that through me He may show His power and that His name might be proclaimed in all the earth. Exodus 9:16.
- The Lord has great plans for me. He plans to prosper me, protect me, and give me hope and a future. Jeremiah 29:11.
- The word of the Lord is right and proper. The Lord is faithful in all He does in my life. Psalms 33:4.
- The Lord makes everything about me beautiful in its time. He has set eternity in my heart so great that it behooves humanity. Ecclesiastes 3:11
- I shall spend my life serving God in my generation. Acts 13:36.
- I shall be strengthened in doing good, for I know I shall reap in time through perseverance. Galatians 6:9.
- I shall lead the life the Lord has assigned me, the life God has called me. 1 Corinthians 7:17.

CLARITY, PERSEVERANCE, AND A PURPOSEFUL LIFE

Be on your guard; stand firm in the faith; be courageous; be strong."
1 Corinthians 16:13

7

THE GREAT MISUNDERSTANDING: POTENTIAL VERSUS PURPOSE

The word potential suggests something existing in possibility, capable of development into actuality, usefulness, and future success. Potentials are so versatile that you can possess many. You may be able to sing, dance, paint, draw, and arrange objects with your hands, or you may be brilliant at your academic studies. You may be able to play musical instruments very well, or you have a way of pulling crowds with your charismatic speeches. You may excel at administrative work, accounting, sales, writing, or public speaking. Athletics may even be your specialty, or you may be doing other skillful tasks with your hands. Individual potential also manifests in aptitudes such as leadership qualities, wisdom, creativity, and compassion. You may be able to do one thing, or you may be able to do several different things, but from the outward standpoint, you have potential.

Potential is referred to in the bible as talents, gifts, abilities, capacities, and capabilities God has endowed each individual. Matthew 25:14-30 tells of the master leaving his house and going on a long journey. He shared his property with his three servants. One got five talents, another two, and the third he gave one. All three servants received according to their abilities. Two servants developed their talents, and the other hid his. Upon the master's return, the two that developed their talent were rewarded, and the one who didn't was cursed and his talent taken away and given to the servant who developed his two talents. From this, the master taught a beneficial lesson that applies to pursuing purpose: more will be given to everyone who develops the talents they were given.

Potentials, therefore, are the human qualities that fuel the individual's desire for growth, development, and achievement. God gives potential to every human being and expects them to use them to develop their lives in ways that will give Him Glory.

You, however, must understand that your potential is externally driven. Your potential is man's purpose for you. They are the things you do that people see and applaud. It is what you do to prove your worth to society to achieve recognition, status, and possession. Your potential allows you to feel a sense of acceptance, inclusivity, connection, and identity among your peers and friends. Your potential enables you to form an identity with the locations you occupy or visit. It is utilizing your skills, abilities, and talents to serve in areas that can allow you to occupy your time and learn valuable lessons and skills essential to building yourself up while building others above you. Your potentials suit the different stages in life in which you go through. Also, for as many experiences as you desire, there is a potential in you that can be cultivated to get you there.

You can pursue and fulfill as many potentials as you desire and serve with your potential for a long time. You can also reap many rewards and success from your potential. However, working at the level of your potential can keep you so busy that you miss your purpose. Over time, if you do not evolve, your potential will become mundane and lack substance. Since the human potential is unique to each individual, gifts, talents, abilities, aptitudes, and capacities cannot be transferred. It, therefore, has no avenue for deposit—it stops with you. This means that functioning to your potential is not a destination; it is your transportation to other and higher levels in life, such as fulfilling your purpose. Fulfilling your purpose is the pinnacle of existence since finding purpose is humanity's deepest desire.

Your potential is not your purpose. While potential and purpose are related, they are not synonymous. In other words, not because you can do something means it is your purpose.

Here's why. Purpose describes why something is created, done, or exists. It is derived from the Anglo-French term *"purpus,"* which means intention, aim, goal, or an object to be kept in view.

In the bible, purpose relates to God's specific reason or mission for each individual. Individuals' purpose is the unique role God has designed for them to fulfill in the universe as a part of His plans. Purpose goes beyond personal success and achievement. The individual's purpose is ultimately about aligning their life with God's will and contributing to His kingdom based on the design God created for them.

Ephesians 2:10 states, "For we are God's handiwork, created in Christ Jesus to do good works, which God prepared in advance for us to do." This tells you that your purpose in life is the very reason you exist, and your purpose is preordained by God, for God, to be carried out by God through you. Therefore, you are a vessel for honorable use. Your obedience in preparing through the use of your potential will determine your qualifications and your capacity to manage the weight of your purpose. Discovering and fulfilling your purpose brings fulfillment, meaning, and a sense of direction to your life. So, you, therefore, must pay the price that comes with you being obedient to achieve the version of yourself that will fulfill your purpose. This will be discussed in the next chapter.

Your purpose is God's way for you to enter the Holy Spirit's workflow in this universe. Purpose shifts your focus from serving others that benefit you to serving others that benefit God's will and desire for humanity and the universe. Purpose moves from generation to generation, creating an impact that causes shifts to awaken the light of courage and inspiration in men. Operating in your purpose inspires others to rise and fight for causes important to them, thereby changing trajectories in their lives to align with God's will for humanity. Purpose seeks fertile soil to plant its seed. It is the defining mark that separates mediocrity from greatness. Operating in your purpose makes you a link in the chain of events of God's work in the grand scheme of His creation. As such, purpose never dies.

Scriptural Affirmations

- I am raised for God to show His power through me, and His name is proclaimed on all the earth. Exodus 9:16.
- I possess the Spirit's manifestation for my generation's common good. 1 Corinthians 12:7.
- The Lord shall lead my heart into the full manifestation of the Love of God and the patient endurance that comes from Christ. 2 Thessalonians 3:5.
- I shall trust the Lord with all my heart and lean on His wisdom. I will submit to the Lord so He can direct my paths to fulfill my purpose. Proverbs 3:5-6.
- I shall commit all I do to the Lord and let Him establish my plans. Proverbs 16:3.
- My talents are natural, easy, and presentable, but I shall endeavor to develop and pursue other areas for greater impact. 1 Corinthians 12:24.
- I shall rise and be strengthened. My purpose shall be fulfilled. Revelations 3:2.
- My faith in the Lord shall allow me to accomplish my purpose in Him. Nothing shall be impossible for me. Matthew 17:20.
- I shall persevere. I shall keep steadfast unless God instructs. 2 Kings 2:24.
- I shall not be complacent. My generation shall not perish. I am here for such a time as this. Esther 4:14.
- I shall do the work of the Lord who sent me while I am able, for there comes a time when I will not be capable. John 9:4.
- My example is that of Jesus Christ. I shall walk in the way of His love, just as He loved me and gave Himself for me as a fragrant offering and sacrifice to God. Ephesians 5:1.

THE HIGH PRICE FOR THE GREAT REWARD

One of the greatest regrets of many elderly individuals is that they did not live a life that was true to their calling. They regret that they never pursued the deepest desires that kept emerging in their heart instead of doing what people expected or what living in a society demanded from them. But, you may ask, *why didn't they do what they felt called to do?* You may even wonder what prevented them. It may be that as you read this chapter, you are feeling the same sentiments of regret.

The answer is a straightforward fact; the price is exceptionally high.

You are intrinsically designed to pursue a sense of safety, security, and status. You want to know that your physical needs are being met, bills can be paid, and your children or lifestyle is taken care of. You want to ensure that you are safe and can trust the people with whom you come in contact. You want to ensure that the possessions you worked hard and sacrificed for are secure, your integrity is intact, and you are praised, honored, and respected for your achievements and growth instead of being criticized for what society may deem a failure. Once you have accomplished your basic needs, it is natural for you to feel a sense of pride and comfort; however, because you are created to grow and evolve continuously, you will always have an itch for more and better as long as you have life. This is where your intrinsic call to purpose stirs.

Putting all you have worked hard for, including the reputation held by others about you, at risk to chase something more and greater seems ridiculous, and it is frowned upon by many, including you. So even if your heart's call is strong, it is drowned or silenced by the fear of what you stand to lose and what others will say.

The Holy Spirit is persistent, and the desire will always haunt you if you choose not to pursue it. Your life will not make sense after a while, and you will constantly be pressured into higher volumes of hardship and pain. Instead of surrendering, you will begin to blame and curse others for your misfortunes. Your fear will consume you as you seek other futile means to satisfy your deep desire to grow and evolve. The rigor of releasing aspects of you that you've known all your life and building the part required to pursue your calling and purpose will scare you. As you have seen in earlier chapters, this process is not easy; many people avoid taking risks and going through difficulties, but it is necessary to please God.

Consider this. Jesus Christ's great purpose on earth was to die as the sacrificial lamb so men could be saved from their sins. With that ultimate purpose in mind, He served as a teacher, master, rabbi, healer, provider, protector, and friend. There came the point where He had to evolve, step up from regular service and life, and enter into His purpose. Jesus knew the price He had to pay and that it would cost Him His life, and He wasn't fazed; however, He was challenged when it came to the appointed time in the Garden of Gethsemane.

During His fasting and praying for the power of God to go through the ordeal that would lead to His death, it is told in the First Corinthians that his anxiety caused His sweat to turn blood. He was faced with the reality that it would be painful and gruesome. He knew what would happen to Him and how He would've been treated. He even asked God to take this cup (His purpose) from Him because the price was too high. But also knowing that not going through with the process would have been much more costly, He prayed, "Yet not my will, but yours be done" (Luke 22:42), as an agreement to surrender fully.

Your purpose is not a matter of talk. Instead, it is a matter of gaining the power of God to accomplish the work He has for you in this earthly realm. Your purpose requires sacrifice, focused energy, and guidance into fruition led by the Holy Spirit. The ordinary things you do, your talents, gifts, and abilities are already what you were created with. Using them is easy, and people love to benefit from the beautiful things you can do with them. Doing them comes with little to no sacrifice or pain to pursue, and you will get carried away, believing it is your purpose. Your purpose, however, requires preparation and divine intervention to be brought to fruition.

Jesus Christ could have been an earthly King. He could have remained a teacher or master, healer, protector, or friend for those in His territory. But instead, He chose the ultimate purpose that God destined for Him.

Jesus's example tells you that through your resolve to accomplish your purpose, which is whatever God has laid on your heart or revealed to you, and through perseverance, you can gain the power you need for your success. To do this, however, you also have a great price you must pay. If it costs you nothing, it will benefit you nothing, and so, the following sacrifices are usually experienced by all individuals who have evolved into their purpose.

Faith

According to Hebrews 11:1, "Faith is the confidence in what we hope for and assurance about what we do not see." With the operative words being *confidence* and *assurance*, faith gives the impression that what you desire exists, but not in your reality and not as yet. Getting what you want requires you to take action. As the scriptures purport, having faith without doing the work amounts to nothing (read James 2:14-26). This is where it gets technical. Getting the opportunity to do the work necessary to achieve your purpose requires you to be vulnerable enough to make sacrifices.

Faith requires you to sacrifice your fears, comfort zones, certainty, control, ego, and pride and cultivate unshakable faith. This may lead you to give up your current job and be unemployed for a season so that you can work on your purpose. You may be required to sell or give away all your possessions and move away from where you live to align with the opportunity for your purpose. You may relocate to start over at different locations for the second, third, or fourth time to align with God's purpose. The Holy Spirit may instruct you to repeatedly give away large sums of money to sow into others, cultivating discipline for the work He has set up for you. You may be required to remain single and alone for a period. You may be required to create or build something for a greater purpose or go into a training program to acquire or improve the requisite skills. You may be required to end friendships and relationships. You may be required to start some friendships and mend broken relationships. You may have to come home from your day job and stay up all night to work on your dream. You must develop discipline by cutting off unhealthy habits and blocking everything that causes distractions. Sacrificing comes with following your heart, which the Holy Spirit guides; therefore, you cannot depend on people's opinions and beliefs. You must trust God.

Faith does not need to be evident to your senses and reasoning to be true. Faith is not an intellectual agreement between you, God, or other people. Faith only requires that you believe in what God has planted in your heart to accomplish. Hebrews 11:6 states, "And without faith, it is impossible to please God because anyone who comes to Him must believe He exists and that He rewards those who earnestly seek Him." We cannot see God with our physical eyes, but we must believe whom He says He is.

Courage

Courage is being bold and confident. It is having the moral strength to do something difficult, possibly dangerous, and makes you afraid. Having courage in God is being confident in the belief that He is who He says He is and will not forsake you because you believe in His word and obey His instructions and guidance. As Moses urges Joshua in Deuteronomy 31:6, "Be strong and courageous. Do not be afraid or terrified because of them, for the Lord your God goes with you; He will never leave you nor forsake you."

To have courage means you must have the mental fortitude to withstand the challenges that arise as you take action by faith. When operating in faith, the things you are called to do will frighten you and others around you. Whatever the case, you will need mental toughness to face the issues that arise and the results, whether they cause you grief, sorrow, pain, or joy. You cannot allow yourself to be carried away by emotions. You must be strong.

You will need the courage to be mentally strong and steadfast when no one believes in you and your desire to pursue your purpose. You will need courage when those you expect to be there for you decide to walk away. You will need courage when your faith leads you to homelessness, hopelessness and to depend on others for food, clothes, and shelter. You will need courage to perform jobs you once considered beneath your desires, abilities, and capabilities. You will need the courage to stay strong and focused when pursuing your purpose causes you to regress for a season. You will need the courage to remain strong when people speak badly about you, criticize, judge, laugh at, mock, and possibly physically and verbally abuse you. You will need the courage to remain faithful when resources get scarce, and you must pause for some time. You will need courage to still believe in God in moments when you experience failure. You will need courage when pursuing your goals looks despairing, and your transformation takes longer than expected. Finally, you will need the courage to be honest with yourself. You will get sad and depressed, and you will cry. However, courage will cause you to stand up, put aside your pride, and face your challenges with confidence and the assurance that your desire will become a reality.

When your desires come to pass, you will need the courage to remain humble as you handle significant responsibilities suddenly assigned to you or steward resources placed in your care.

Every stage of your purpose journey requires you to have the courage to endure. You are God's chosen vessel. He needs you to fulfill His purpose on earth for which you were created. It is only through your obedience that you can experience fulfillment.

Isolation

Faith and courage to pursue what God has laid on your heart will cause you to be alone for a season. People will not believe in you and your purpose journey at first. They will reject your plans and ideas and will chastise you. They will not want to stand with you or want to identify with you. It is not a personal attack against you; it is God's way of letting you know they are not aligned with your purpose and may not be able to accompany you on the next leg of your journey. It is a sad occasion, but your courage strengthens as you journey alone and in isolation.

To be isolated means to remain alone or to be separated from others, physically and otherwise.

The Bible warns against the dangers of isolation; however, in some instances, it gives examples of the importance of isolation. This means isolation must only be done when God initiates it.

Isolation helps you distance yourself from your present circumstances so you can think objectively about your past, where you are, and your prospective future. It allows you to look at your character, location, and the people and things you surround yourself with to have a proper strategy and requisite tools to develop yourself for the future God has placed in your heart.

God uses isolation to develop your spiritual capacity and character. Isolation helps you to hear God clearly, and depend on His guidance for survival and sustenance. You learn to wait for His instructions and to have a sense of security in His protection and provision as you endure. This causes you to have greater understanding and discernment. Wisdom and insight help build your character.

Through character development, you see your deficiencies, weaknesses, insecurities and how much control you try to exert in the flow of life. In isolation, God allows you to be broken and vulnerable so that He can rebuild you and prepare you for purpose. As a result, your pride will be removed and replaced with humility. Humility is a life of total surrender to God, where you acknowledge that all you do and acquire are only by the grace of God where, like Job, no matter what you are blessed with, you can easily say, "… The Lord gave, and the Lord has taken away; may the name of the Lord be praised", (Job 1:21).

Isolation is a scary part of your journey. You may become upset with those you love and care about for not being there for you or helping you. You may get upset with God for abandoning you in times when He gets silent. God is omnipresent. He is way ahead of you even when He is present with you (Deuteronomy 31:8). This is confirmation that He knows where He is directing and taking you. Isolation is God's gift to prepare you for your next level.

Perseverance

Perseverance brings this topic, the high price for a great reward, into a full circle, with faith being the foundation. When you believe in the purpose God has laid on your heart and the conviction that it is the correct thing to do, you will pursue it. Your courage to withstand persecution, and endure a season of isolation, will help you to keep going when you get stuck, when the plans you're pursuing don't work according to your expectation, and when the goalpost to achieve your goals keeps moving. You will persevere when partners or supporters have neglected you and when God gets silent on you.

Perseverance helps you change and adapt in whatever way your goals require to get you through difficult and uncertain times. It stretches you beyond your ideals and causes you to learn more about your strengths and capabilities. Perseverance sometimes comes with blood, sweat, and tears. It is tough. But it's a sacrifice to make to fulfill your purpose.

Usually, most purpose seekers give up on their journey when they realize the price they must pay. However, your ability to persevere will set you apart. Like the woman with the issue of blood (Luke 8:43-48), her faith and ability to persevere took virtue, otherwise called power, from Jesus's body. Power is the great reward you receive after paying a high price.

Receiving the power of God sincerely cements your belief in Jesus Christ, yourself, and your place in this universe. You release resistance, control, and attachments and allow life to flow. Barriers and changes in the times and seasons do not limit you or cause you anxiety. You are confident in your ability to live in this world no matter what life throws your way. Your ego does not rule you; you avoid judging others and their actions. You avoid conflicts, competition, and compromising situations. You do not need to prove anything to anyone. You become open-minded and willingly participate in activities for growth, whether work or play. You have no resistance to communicating with people from different educational and socioeconomic backgrounds, for you are unaffected by an inferiority complex. You are confident in yourself, and the obstacles you have courageously overcome give you high self-esteem. You become both a teacher and a teachable individual, humble in all your ways and resilient.

Your source of happiness comes from within. External forces do not influence you. You live with a sense of freedom, and the peace of God governs and guides your life. You have a heightened sense of awareness of yourself and your environment. You live with a deep understanding of gratitude and engage life on your terms. With the humility you cultivated, you can see, accept and appreciate the bigger picture of life. You easily transcend the self and accept life for what it is, and as such, you become non-discriminatory, knowing everyone is doing their best with what they have and know.

In this, you will know true love as outlined in 1 Corinthians 13:4-8, "Love is patient, love is kind. It does not envy; it does not boast; it is not proud. It does not dishonor others; it is not self-seeking; it is not easily angered; it keeps no record of wrongs. Love does not delight in evil but rejoices with the truth. It always protects, always trusts, hopes, and always perseveres. Love never fails."

All things negative stem from pride, while growth and advancement are found in love. Therefore, paying the price allows you to transcend to higher levels of unchanging, unconditional, and permanent love filled with true joy, peace, and illumination, a state that every believer should aspire to attain instead of going to their graves with regret.

Scriptural Affirmations

- I shall be strong and courageous, for I am destined to lead people to the inheritance the Lord had sworn to their ancestors to give them. Joshua 1:6.
- I shall stand my guard. I shall stand firm in my faith. I am courageous, and I am strong. 1 Corinthians 16:3.
- I shall fear the Lord and serve Him with all faithfulness. I shall discard anything and everything that stands in the way of my service to God. Joshua 24:14.
- My knowledge of Jesus Christ, obedience, and service to Him are worth more than anything or anyone I could ever lose. Philippians 3:8.
- I can do all things through Christ, who gives me strength. Philippians 4:13.
- My success and fulfillment come from the Spirit of the Lord Almighty. Zechariah 4:6.
- No weapon formed against me shall prosper. Every tongue that rises against me in judgment shall be condemned. Isaiah 54:17.
- The grace of the Lord is sufficient to keep me, for His strength is perfect in my weakness. I shall gladly boast about my weakness so that the power of Christ may rest on me. 2 Corinthians 12:9
- I am the epitome of God's heart. I shall do everything the Lord desires me to do. Acts 13:22.
- I have a divine, pre-ordained purpose that is set by the Lord Jesus Christ to be fulfilled. I, therefore, put aside everything that stands in the way of my purpose and endeavor to do the work established for me. Hebrews 12:1-2.

- I shall devote my life to doing the work of the Lord, which gives substance even into eternity, for it is only on the Lord that God has given His approval. John 6:27.
- My present suffering shall not be compared with the glory that shall be revealed in me. Romans 8:18.

A PURPOSEFUL LIFE

Life is all about beginnings and endings. In Revelations 22:13, God refers to Himself as "the Alpha and the Omega, the First and the Last, the Beginning and the End." This verse indicates that God is the God of beginnings as He was in the beginning, and He is the God of endings, referring to the fact that He brings all things to their determined end. God is the creator; He brings humanity into existence and removes them according to His timing. This means our life will end at some point in the journey of existence.

The problem with many of us is that when we consider our mortality, we are overcome with fear. We try our best to hide or bury the thought of death with distractions and incessantly bad habits. We may have desires we want to fulfill but need time or are afraid to be separated from our loved ones. We may be afraid to be exposed to living a life that is not up to the standard we constantly desire, or we lack the courage to pursue our purposeful life; therefore, we bargain for more time.

Unless death is deliberately achieved by suicide, death warns no one. It comes when God says it's time. To deny death is to deny our life since death is as much part of our journey as life. Therefore, we must live with our eminent death at the forefront of our minds.

To accept death is to accept that life is a gift that must be lived purposefully. To accept death is to get that life is the gateway to doing meaningful things that will fill our souls while impacting others. Death must inspire us to live, not from the dictates of our circumstances, the pressure from societal trends and people in our circle, but from the place in our hearts where God placed His vision for us. We must have the determination and resolve to live the life we were called and convicted to live on this earth, no matter how painful and shameful segments in our life may have been. We must let our pain and adversity fuel our determination to fulfill our purpose. Use the lessons from our pain and life experiences to crush the serpent's head and leave a legacy for those whose heals it will bruise after we've passed away.

How do you live a purposeful life, you may ask?

At this very moment, be honest with yourself about the vision God gave you for your life. Life is fleeting; therefore, you should endeavor to surrender that vision back to God and faithfully allow the Holy Spirit to guide you into its fulfillment.

It will not be easy, but as Jesus prayed to God in the garden of Gethsemane, "Father, if you are willing, take this cup from me; yet not my will, but yours be done" (Luke 22:42). Do what you are called to do instead of resisting. Leave the outcome to God. God created you; He knows and sees you exactly as He made you, not as your life circumstances or the world dictates. Flow with His guidance. Wherever He leads, follow. Whatever season He puts you to rest in, remain without complaining. Whatever He tells you to do, do it.

As you follow the leading of the Holy Spirit, you will embark on your quest to pursue and fulfill your purpose. You will be guided into creating real, physical, lasting, and impactful change. Like Moses, you may not feel qualified, but God will give you courage and help and never leave you. You will have free access to communicate with God through the Holy Spirit.

With certainty yet unpredictability of your death, you do not have time to waste. Make every moment count. Seek to love as Christ loves, forgive as Christ forgives, be bold and courageous, and take action as

Christ did. Focus on what you are genuinely and intrinsically inspired to do to bring yourself true joy and fulfillment while impacting others.

Don't get stuck in cycles and situations that cause you to suffer purposelessly. This will only cause bitterness, sorrow, regret, fear, hatred, anger, envy, jealousy, shame, guilt, and apathy to take residence in your heart. Instead, pursue your goals, dreams, visions, friendships, and the relationship you intrinsically desire. Then, enjoy them to the glory of God, knowing nothing lasts forever.

Understand that you are a link in the chain of purpose, don't let the chain falter because of your fear and unbelief. Instead, adjust your perspective by utilizing the available resources such as prayer, meditation, spiritual counseling, and psychotherapy to learn the lessons from the experiences and improve. At the end of your life, you should be able to say, like Paul, "I have fought the good fight, I have finished the race, I have kept the faith. Now there is in store for me the crown of righteousness, which the Lord, the righteous judge, will award me on that day" (2 Timothy 4:7-8).

Answering the call of God, finding and fulfilling your purpose, and living a purposeful life is the opportunity you get to finish this life well, leaving an impact that will be remembered for eternity.

Scriptural Affirmations

- I am prosperous and safe in the Lord. I have hope. I have a future. Jeremiah 29:11.
- I am zealous. I am spiritually fervent in serving the Lord. Romans 12:11.
- The divine power of the Holy Spirit has given me everything I need for a Godly life through my knowledge of His glory and goodness. 2 Peter 1:3.
- I commend the work of the Lord; I declare all His mighty acts to the next generation. Psalm 145:4.
- Everything I do, whether in word or deed, I do them in the name of the Lord Jesus, and I give thanks to God the Father through Jesus Christ. Colossians 3:17.
- I plant seeds of goodness in this world, and the Lord makes them grow. 1 Corinthians 3:6.
- I am here in this season to preserve a remnant that will save lives by a great deliverance. Genesis 45:7.
- This is my time and season to do what the Lord has called me to do. Ecclesiastes 3:1.
- I love the Lord. I am called according to His purpose. All things are working together for my good. Romans 8:28.
- I trust the plans of the Lord with all my heart. Proverbs 19:21.
- The love of the Lord surpasses all knowledge. I am filled to the measure of all the goodness of God. Ephesians 3:19.
- The world and all things within it will fade. But whoever does the will of God lives forever. 1 John 2:17

FINAL THOUGHTS

It's Your Choice

If you desire to change and experience the joy of being purposeful and impactful in each moment, you must decide to take authority over your life. Jesus Christ is your creator. He gives you the free will to partner with Him to take your life to a higher level. He has given you great desires to fulfill, and He wants to empower you to accomplish them. Your ability to fulfill your purpose adds to the bigger picture of creation and God's purpose for humanity. You are much more important and significant to God and His creation than you can fathom. Understanding and accepting this will shift your mindset and your choices.

Life is a journey. Many people take it so seriously that they get wrapped up in daily chaos from news bulletins, social media, celebrity gossip, economic and health crisis, fashion trends, influencer marketing, peer gossiping, and more. When you immerse yourself in the chaos, living in the alignment of whom Jesus Christ created you to be is impossible. You can choose to take a stand. You can shift from the chaos and focus on your identity and purpose in Jesus Christ. You can decide to establish your life on the premise of the truth of Jesus Christ instead of subscribing to the constant chaos in the world.

You have been given this beautiful gift of life. Your deepest desire is to experience this gift in a way that brings you ease and joy. It is, therefore, up to you to decide to get into alignment with your deepest desires. Life is not easy, and I am not submitting the idea to you that it is. You will experience dark, challenging, and painful seasons but also blissful moments filled with fun, success, and laughter. Your perspective is integral in navigating each season to create balance so you can remain aligned with who you divinely are. Suffering and pain cultivate character in you. It is the substance you need to grow, mature, and develop in God.

Life is about experiencing, learning, growing, evolving, and sharing your wisdom throughout the journey. Living is possible if you partner with the right source, Jesus Christ. You can choose to do it Jesus's way by surrendering to the knowledge that He desires what is best for you and freeing yourself of the chaos and misfortunes of this world. You will find that all energy and positive forces in life will join to ensure your dreams and desires to impact and live a purposeful life await you.

The Believer's Life

Your purpose is love. Let us love one another, for love is of God, and everyone who loves is born of God and knows God.

Urgently answer your call. Diligently accept the Caller. Both are crucial to your growth and protection from the enemy of your soul and purpose. The enemy, the thief, comes only to steal, kill, and destroy. The Caller has come that you may have life and have it complete.

Therefore, get clarity. Persevere. Be on your guard—stand firm in the faith. Be courageous. Be strong. Live a purposeful life so you fulfill the faith to which you were called.

Notes

Chapter 4

The definition of *call* and how it was used to establish my understanding and intent (page 11).

https://www.merriam-webster.com/dictionary/call

Chapter 6

The origin and meaning of the word *thought* and how it has evolved. It also tells how it applies to the topic (page 17).

https://www.etymonline.com/word/thought

Chapter 7

The origin and meaning of the word *purpose* and how it was used to develop my understanding (page 25).

https://www.etymonline.com/word/purpose

If this book has been a blessing, we would love to hear about it. Please send your comments about this book to our publishers at the address below.

Write to: vp35pluspub@gmail.com